W9-AVX-553

Tools

Search

Notes

Discuss
MyReportLinks.com Books

Go!

STATES

VERMONT

A MyReportLinks.com Book

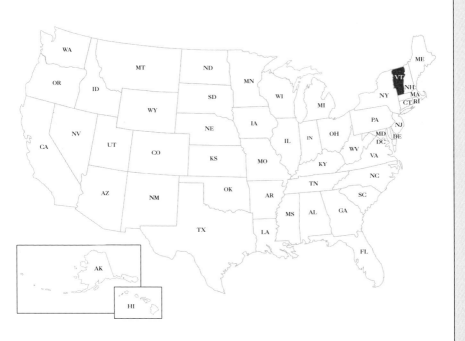

David Schaffer

MyReportLinks.com Books
an imprint of

Enslow Publishers, Inc.

Box 398, 40 Industrial Road
Berkeley Heights, NJ 07922
USA

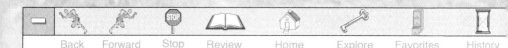
To my Mom and Dad,
for the time we have spent together in Vermont.

MyReportLinks.com Books, an imprint of Enslow Publishers, Inc. MyReportLinks is a trademark of Enslow Publishers, Inc.

Library of Congress Cataloging-in-Publication Data

Schaffer, David.
Vermont / David Schaffer.
    p. cm. — (States)
Summary: Discusses the land and climate, economy, government, and history of the state of Vermont. Includes Internet links to Web sites.
  Includes bibliographical references and index.
  ISBN 0-7660-5110-2
  1. Vermont—Juvenile literature. [1. Vermont.] I. Title. II. States (Series : Berkeley Heights, N.J.)
F49.3 .S33 2003
974.3—dc21

                          2002003417

Printed in the United States of America

10 9 8 7 6 5 4 3 2 1

To Our Readers:
Through the purchase of this book, you and your library gain access to the Report Links that specifically back up this book.
The Publisher will provide access to the Report Links that back up this book and will keep these Report Links up to date on **www.myreportlinks.com** for three years from the book's first publication date.
We have done our best to make sure all Internet addresses in this book were active and appropriate when we went to press. However, the author and the Publisher have no control over, and assume no liability for, the material available on those Internet sites or on other Web sites they may link to.
The usage of the MyReportLinks.com Books Web site is subject to the terms and conditions stated on the Usage Policy Statement on **www.myreportlinks.com**.
In the future, a password may be required to access the Report Links that back up this book. The password is found on the bottom of page 4 of this book.
Any comments or suggestions can be sent by e-mail to comments@myreportlinks.com or to the address on the back cover.

Photo Credits: America's Story from America's Library/Library of Congress, pp. 27, 35; American Memory/Library of Congress, p. 19; Ben & Jerry's Homemade Holdings, Inc., pp. 13, 24; © Corel Corporation, pp. 3, 21, 34, 44; © 1995 PhotoDisc, p. 11; © 1999 PhotoDisc, p. 23; © 1999 Corbis Corp., p. 12; Enslow Publishers, Inc., pp. 18, 38, 39; foliage-vermont.com, p. 28; gorptravel.com, p. 30; Library of Congress, pp. 3 (Constitution), 42; MyReportLinks.com Books, p. 4; New Perspectives on the West/PBS, p. 16; State of Vermont: Office of the Governor, p. 33; Trapp Family Lodge, p. 14; University of Vermont, p. 40; Vermont Apples, p. 26.

Cover Photo: ©1999 PhotoDisc

Cover Description: Farm in Vermont Valley.

Contents

MyReportLinks.com Books
Great Books, Great Links, Great for Research!

MyReportLinks.com Books present the information you need to learn about your report subject. In addition, they show you where to go on the Internet for more information. The pre-evaluated Report Links that back up this book are kept up to date on **www.myreportlinks.com**. With the purchase of a MyReportLinks.com Books title, you and your library gain access to the Report Links that specifically back up that book. The Report Links save hours of research time and link to dozens—even hundreds—of Web sites, source documents, and photos related to your report topic.

Please see "To Our Readers" on the Copyright page for important information about this book, the MyReportLinks.com Books Web site, and the Report Links that back up this book.

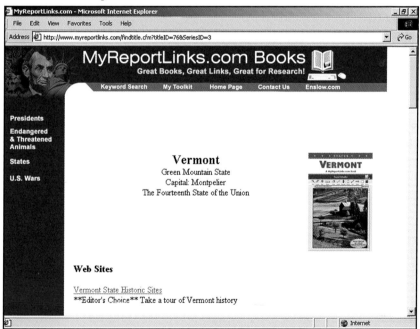

Access:

The Publisher will provide access to the Report Links that back up this book and will try to keep these Report Links up to date on our Web site for three years from the book's first publication date. Please enter **SVT7196** if asked for a password.

Report Links

 The Internet sites described below can be accessed at
http://www.myreportlinks.com

*EDITOR'S CHOICE

▶ **Vermont State Historic Sites**
Vermont State Historic Sites Web site explores significant historic
places in Vermont. These include the Bennington Battle Monument,
Calvin Coolidge's boyhood home, and Hyde Log Cabin, one of the
oldest log cabins in the nation.

Link to this Internet site from http://www.myreportlinks.com

*EDITOR'S CHOICE

▶ **Vermont: Green Mountain State**
At this Web site you will find links to facts and information about the
state of Vermont.

Link to this Internet site from http://www.myreportlinks.com

*EDITOR'S CHOICE

▶ **Explore the States: Vermont**
America's Story from America's Library, a Library of Congress Web site,
tells the story of Vermont. Here you will learn basic facts about the
state and find interesting stories about Vermont's history.

Link to this Internet site from http://www.myreportlinks.com

*EDITOR'S CHOICE

▶ **U.S. Census Bureau: Vermont**
At this Web site you will find the official census on the state of
Vermont. Learn about the state's commerce, geography, population
demographics, and more.

Link to this Internet site from http://www.myreportlinks.com

*EDITOR'S CHOICE

▶ **Vermont State Parks: Just for Kids**
At this Web site you can explore Vermont's state parks. Here you will
find fun activities as well as informative descriptions of parks such as
Boulder Beach, Crystal Lake, and others.

Link to this Internet site from http://www.myreportlinks.com

*EDITOR'S CHOICE

▶ **Vermont Historical Society Museum**
This online exhibit about Vermont's history includes a collection of
historic portraits and images documenting the history of Vermont's
State House. You will also find an online exhibit dedicated to Vermont's
history from 1820 to 1850.

Link to this Internet site from http://www.myreportlinks.com

 The Internet sites described below can be accessed at
http://www.myreportlinks.com

▶ **All Natural Ben & Jerry's: Vermont's Finest**
At the official Ben & Jerry's Web site you can learn all about "Vermont's Finest" ice cream. Learn the history of this Vermont-based company and about their latest flavors.

Link to this Internet site from http://www.myreportlinks.com

▶ **American Masters—Norman Rockwell**
Although he was not a native Vermonter, Norman Rockwell lived in Vermont for many years. This PBS Web site contains a brief profile of Rockwell's life, art, and legacy.

Link to this Internet site from http://www.myreportlinks.com

▶ **Brigham Young**
PBS's "New Perspectives on The West" profiles Vermont native Brigham Young. He became the leader of the Church of Jesus Christ of Latter-day Saints, also known as the Mormon Church.

Link to this Internet site from http://www.myreportlinks.com

▶ **Destination: Vermont**
This Web site provides brief descriptions of destinations in Vermont. Here you will learn about Vermont's outdoor attractions, Green Mountain National Park, Vermont's ski resorts, and the beautiful foliage the state is known for.

Link to this Internet site from http://www.myreportlinks.com

▶ **Ethan Allen History**
This biography of Ethan Allen discusses his involvement with the Green Mountain boys, his time spent fighting in the American Revolution, his role in the Republic of Vermont, and his legacy.

Link to this Internet site from http://www.myreportlinks.com

▶ **foliage-vermont.com**
Discover the leaves of Vermont at foliage-vermont.com. Native legends, and scientific reasons as to why leaves change color are discussed.

Link to this Internet site from http://www.myreportlinks.com

Report Links

 The Internet sites described below can be accessed at
http://www.myreportlinks.com

▶ The Friends of Robert Frost
This Web site is dedicated to Robert Frost's life and work. His biography, a chronology of his life, photographs, and poems are included. You will also find information about the poet's house in Shaftsbury, Vermont.

Link to this Internet site from http://www.myreportlinks.com

▶ The Gentleman Boss President
This Web site contains a comprehensive biography of Vermont native, Chester A. Arthur. An image gallery, quotes, and additional links are provided.

Link to this Internet site from http://www.myreportlinks.com

▶ George Dewey
This biography of Vermont native Admiral George Dewey includes information about his life and career. A lot of attention is paid to his role in the Spanish-American War.

Link to this Internet site from http://www.myreportlinks.com

▶ Joseph Smith
At this Web site you will find the biography of Joseph Smith, the founder of the Church of Jesus Christ of Latter-day Saints. Here you will learn about his youth, authorship of *The Book of Mormon*, the growth of Mormonism, his bid for presidency, and his murder.

Link to this Internet site from http://www.myreportlinks.com

▶ Lake Champlain Maritime Museum
This section of the Lake Champlain Maritime Museum contains facts about the American Indians of the region, military history, commerce history, and twentieth-century history. You will also find information about places to visit.

Link to this Internet site from http://www.myreportlinks.com

▶ The Passive President
A comprehensive biography of former president and Vermont native Calvin Coolidge. It includes an image gallery, quotes, and additional links.

Link to this Internet site from http://www.myreportlinks.com

Report Links

 The Internet sites described below can be accessed at
http://www.myreportlinks.com

▶ **Rutland Herald**
Get the local news from one of Vermont's leading newspapers,
the *Rutland Herald.* Here you will learn about the state's local sports,
businesses, and much more.

Link to this Internet site from http://www.myreportlinks.com

▶ **Samuel de Champlain and New France**
This Web site provides the original seventeenth-century maps of New England
drawn by explorer Samuel de Champlain.

Link to this Internet site from http://www.myreportlinks.com

▶ **Stately Knowledge: Vermont**
Did you know that Vermont does not have any professional sports teams? At
this Web site you will learn interesting facts about Vermont and find
additional online resources and helpful links.

Link to this Internet site from http://www.myreportlinks.com

▶ **Today In History: A Constitution for Vermont**
By navigating through this page you will find a brief history of Vermont's
constitution. You will also learn about local traditions and find images
of Vermonters.

Link to this Internet site from http://www.myreportlinks.com

▶ **The Trapp Family Museum**
Explore the history of *The Sound of Music,* the family behind the production,
and their connection to Vermont.

Link to this Internet site from http://www.myreportlinks.com

▶ **Vermont Apples**
Did you know that the McIntosh is the most abundant apple in Vermont?
Learn this and other interesting facts about Vermont's apple industry.

Link to this Internet site from http://www.myreportlinks.com

Report Links

 The Internet sites described below can be accessed at
http://www.myreportlinks.com

▶ **The Vermont Environmental Board: Act 250**
This page contains the text of Vermont's Land Use and Development
law, an influential piece of legislation.

Link to this Internet site from http://www.myreportlinks.com

▶ **Vermont Explorer**
This Web site provides information about vacationing in Vermont.
Here you will learn about attractions, nature, recreation, and much more.

Link to this Internet site from http://www.myreportlinks.com

▶ **Vermont's Great Moments of the 20th Century**
This brief biography about Senator George Aiken discusses his thirty-
four years of service in the United States Senate. He was known for
championing the rights of the common man.

Link to this Internet site from http://www.myreportlinks.com

▶ **Vermont State History**
This Web site contains a brief history of Vermont. You will also find
information about geography, tourism, and outdoor life in Vermont.

Link to this Internet site from http://www.myreportlinks.com

▶ **Vermont Secretary of State's Kid Page**
The state of Vermont has six elective offices. At this Web site you can
learn what they are and who holds them. Information about Vermont's
geography, history, and state symbols is also included.

Link to this Internet site from http://www.myreportlinks.com

▶ **Wilson A. Bentley**
This page provides a brief biography of Wilson A. Bentley, the man who
proved that no two snowflakes are alike.

Link to this Internet site from http://www.myreportlinks.com

Vermont Facts

Capital
Montpelier

Population
608,827*

Bird
Hermit thrush

Tree
Sugar maple

Flower
Red clover

Animal
Morgan horse

Fish
Brook trout and walleye pike

Insect
Honeybee

Mineral
Talc

Gemstone
Grossular garnet

Song
"These Green Mountains"
(composed by Diane Martin;
arranged by Rita Buglass.)

Motto
Freedom and Unity

Flag
A pine tree sits in the center of a wilderness scene with wild animals in a surrounding field. Blue mountains appear behind the field. A green wreath surrounds the wilderness scene, and the profile of a reindeer sits above it. Below, the state motto, "Freedom and Unity," appears on either side of the state name. These images are against a dark blue background.

Nickname
Green Mountain State

Gained Statehood
March 4, 1791,
the fourteenth state

Counties
14

Population reflects the 2000 census.

The Green Mountain State

Vermont is a small, mountainous state tucked away in the northwest corner of New England. It covers only 9,600 square miles and ranks forty-third among the fifty states in size. The population, 608,827, is also small—only Wyoming has fewer people.[1] The Green Mountains, part of the Appalachian Range, run down the middle of the state. The high elevations make Vermont winters cold. Forests cover more than 75 percent of the state. Two thirds of Vermont's residents live in rural areas, the highest

▲ Over 75 percent of Vermont is covered with breathtaking forests. Tourists travel to the state during the autumn months to catch a glimpse of the beautiful leaves.

▲ *There are still a number of small farms in Vermont. The state is famous for its dairy products.*

proportion of any state. The largest city is Burlington, with a population of about forty thousand. Other cities are Barre, Bennington, Brattleboro, Rutland, St. Johnsbury, and the capital, Montpelier.

▶ What is Special About Vermont?

Vermont is known for a variety of products and industries. Quarrying for minerals, especially granite and marble, has been an important industry. Vermont marble was used in the U.S. Supreme Court building and in the Jefferson Memorial. Slate, talc, and asbestos have also been mined in Vermont.

Agriculture is also an important part of Vermont's economy. Vermont is the main supplier of milk to the city of Boston as well as other cities and towns in southern New England and upstate New York. Vermont cheeses, especially cheddar cheese, are sold around the world. Other major agricultural products include apple cider, fruit preserves, honey, jams, jellies, and maple syrup.

Many people think of Vermont as a state for winter sports. The first ski tow in the United States was introduced in the state in 1933. Since then, Vermont has become one of the most popular places to go skiing in the world. Other winter sports, including snowmobiling and snowboarding, and nature activities, such as boating, camping, and hiking also attract visitors.

▲ *Ben Cohen and Jerry Greenfield cofounded Ben & Jerry's Ice Cream in Burlington, Vermont.*

Other tourists like to spend time in Vermont's quaint inns and villages, enjoying the beautiful scenery. The wooded hillsides are especially pretty when the leaves change colors in autumn.

Not all of Vermont's products are traditional. New exports include gourmet coffee from Green Mountain Coffee Roasters and teddy bears from the Vermont Teddy Bear Company. Probably the most famous Vermont businessmen are Ben Cohen and Jerry Greenfield, who started Ben & Jerry's Ice Cream. In addition to offering new and unusual flavors, Ben & Jerry's was popular for showing movies on the outside wall of its first parlor.

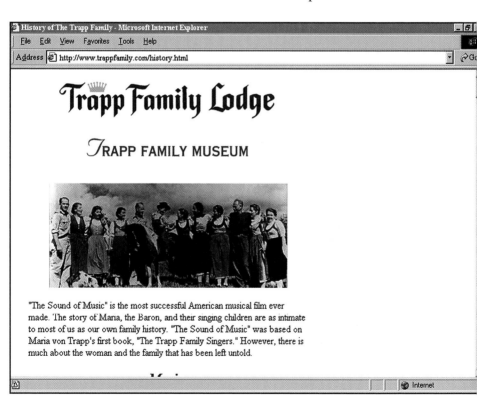

The von Trapp family, famous for the musical The Sound of Music, moved to Stowe, Vermont, after fleeing from Austria during World War II.

Famous and Important Vermonters

Two American presidents came from Vermont. Chester A. Arthur served from 1881 to 1885. Calvin Coolidge served from 1923 to 1929.

George Aiken was a Vermont governor and also a U.S. senator for more than thirty years. He was one of the first government officials to speak out against the Vietnam War in the 1960s and 1970s. In 2001, Vermont Senator Jim Jeffords caused a stir when he switched from being a Republican to an independent. This meant that the Democrats gained control of the U.S. Senate.

Many artists, writers, and musical performers were either born in Vermont or moved to the state. Nineteenth-century sculptor Larkin Mead, who created the sculptures on Abraham Lincoln's tomb, came from Vermont. Poet Robert Frost and artist Norman Rockwell both lived there for a time. The state's beauty and character helped to inspire some of their greatest work.

Rudy Vallee, a well-known singer in the 1950s and 1960s, came from Vermont. The von Trapp family, made famous by the movie *The Sound of Music*, settled in Stowe after fleeing from Austria during World War II.

Vermont has always been home to people with new ideas about society. George Marsh introduced the idea of land and nature preservation in his 1864 book *Man and Nature*.

Vermonters also believe that education is very important. Burlington native John Dewey, perhaps America's most famous philosopher, was very interested in education. He believed it was important to combine learning in the class-room with practical experience in the real world. Dewey's ideas are now widely accepted in schools and other learn-ing institutions in many countries.

Back   Forward   Stop   Review   Home   Explore   Favorites   History

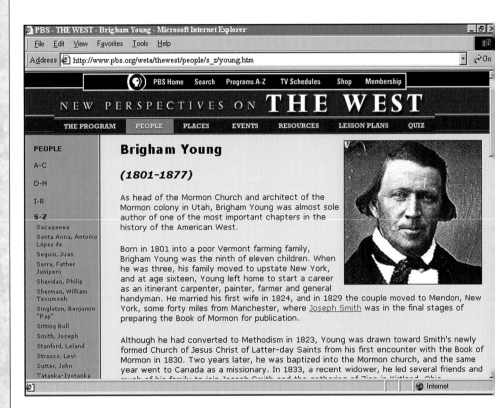

File   Edit   View   Favorites   Tools   Help

Address   http://www.pbs.org/weta/thewest/people/s_z/young.htm   Go

PBS Home   Search   Programs A-Z   TV Schedules   Shop   Membership

NEW PERSPECTIVES ON THE WEST

THE PROGRAM   PEOPLE   PLACES   EVENTS   RESOURCES   LESSON PLANS   QUIZ

PEOPLE

A-C

D-H

I-R

S-Z

Sacagawea
Santa Anna, Antonio
López de
Seguin, Juan
Serra, Father
Junipero
Sheridan, Philip
Sherman, William
Tecumseh
Singleton, Benjamin
"Pap"
Sitting Bull
Smith, Joseph
Stanford, Leland
Strauss, Levi
Sutter, John
Tatanka-Iyotanka

Brigham Young

(1801-1877)

As head of the Mormon Church and architect of the Mormon colony in Utah, Brigham Young was almost sole author of one of the most important chapters in the history of the American West.

Born in 1801 into a poor Vermont farming family, Brigham Young was the ninth of eleven children. When he was three, his family moved to upstate New York, and at age sixteen, Young left home to start a career as an itinerant carpenter, painter, farmer and general handyman. He married his first wife in 1824, and in 1829 the couple moved to Mendon, New York, some forty miles from Manchester, where Joseph Smith was in the final stages of preparing the Book of Mormon for publication.

Although he had converted to Methodism in 1823, Young was drawn toward Smith's newly formed Church of Jesus Christ of Latter-day Saints from his first encounter with the Book of Mormon in 1830. Two years later, he was baptized into the Mormon church, and the same year went to Canada as a missionary. In 1833, a recent widower, he led several friends and

Internet

▲ *Brigham Young, one of the founders of the Mormon Church (officially called the Church of Jesus Christ of Latter-day Saints) was a Vermont native.*

Some Vermont natives have made names for themselves after they left the state. Joseph Smith and Brigham Young, the founders of the Church of Jesus Christ of Latter-day Saints, moved west to Utah. William G. Wilson and Robert Holbrook Smith were living in New York and Ohio when they started the self-help group Alcoholics Anonymous. People such as these have helped the small state of Vermont make a big impression on America and the rest of the world.

Land and Climate

The Canadian province of Quebec borders Vermont to the north. New Hampshire lies to the east, across the Connecticut River. Massachusetts is to the south and New York to the west. Lake Champlain and the Poultney River form more than half of the western border.

▶ Degrees of Cold

Vermont's northern location and high elevation give it a cold climate. The average winter temperature is about 20°F. The record low is −50°F. The state averages about seventy-five inches of snow a year, but the highest mountains often receive more than one hundred inches. There are four regions in Vermont: the lowlands, the central mountain region, the eastern foothills, and the northeast highlands. Their climates vary, mostly in terms of temperature.

The lowlands are in the northwestern part of the state. The Champlain Valley, which includes the state's largest city, Burlington, is located here. This region is milder than most of the state, mostly because of its lower elevation. Temperatures throughout the year are usually a few degrees warmer here than in the coldest regions.

The central mountain region has the highest elevations and the harshest winter weather. The cities of Bennington, Montpelier, and Rutland are in this region. The northeast highlands are the most thickly-forested part of Vermont. Wildlife here includes bears, elks, and moose. St. Johnsbury and Newport are the largest towns in this area.

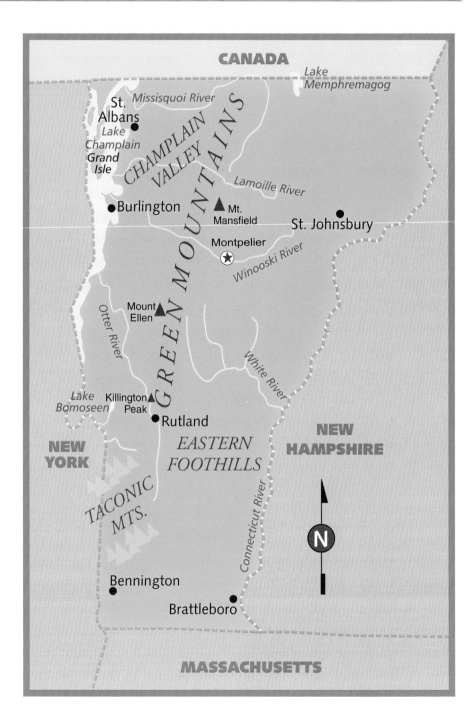

CANADA

Lake Memphremagog

St. Albans

Missisquoi River

Lake Champlain

Grand Isle

CHAMPLAIN VALLEY

Lamoille River

Burlington

Mt. Mansfield

St. Johnsbury

Montpelier ⭐

Winooski River

GREEN MOUNTAINS

Otter River

Mount Ellen

White River

Lake Bomoseen

Killington Peak

Rutland

EASTERN FOOTHILLS

NEW YORK

TACONIC MTS.

NEW HAMPSHIRE

Connecticut River

N

Bennington

Brattleboro

MASSACHUSETTS

▲ A map of Vermont.

Tools   Search   Notes   Discuss   Go!

American Memory Digital Item Display - fsa1992001241/PP - Microsoft Internet Explorer

File   Edit   View   Favorites   Tools   Help

Address em/fsaall:@filreq(@field(NUMBER+@band(fsac+1a34559))+@field(COLLID+fsac)):displayType=1:m856sd=fsac:m856sf=   Go

Digital ID: fsac 1a34559 Source: intermediate roll film
Retrieve uncompressed archival TIFF version (663 kilobytes)

Done   Internet

In Vermont, farms like this one are found in the western and southeastern parts of the state.

East of the Green Mountains and south of the White River are the eastern foothills. Like the northwest lowlands, these foothills have milder conditions. Brattleboro is the largest city in this region.

Although winters are cold, the summers in Vermont can get warm, sometimes hot. In July and August, the temperature frequently reaches 90°F in the northwestern lowlands and the southern valleys. Even in the cold northern mountains, high temperatures reach into the 80s during these months. Overall, Vermont's average

summer temperature is about 70°F. The record high is 105°F. Spring in Vermont can be damp and chilly. Thawing snow and ice combine with spring rain in March and April to make "Mud Season." During this time, much of the ground becomes a thick layer of mud. In the rural areas it can become difficult to get around without a four-wheel-drive vehicle.

The majority of Vermont's crops are grown in the low-lying western valleys and the southeast. Dairy farms are found mostly in the south and the northeast valleys. The mineral mining and quarrying industries are based in the central mountains. Most of the winter resorts are also found there. Lumbering and milling take place mostly in the northeast foothills.

▶ The Effects of Glaciers

About twenty-five thousand years ago, giant glaciers covered most of Vermont. The mountain peaks then reached as high as fifteen thousand feet. Erosion from flowing ice cut them down dramatically. The highest mountains in Vermont are now Mount Mansfield at 4,393 feet, Killington at 4,241 feet, and Mount Ellen at 4,135 feet.

The glaciers also created deep valleys. Major river valleys include those of the Champlain, Connecticut, Lamoille, White, and Winooski rivers. The nincty-mile-long Otter Creek, which flows into Lake Champlain from the south, is Vermont's longest river.

The glaciers also left many smaller bodies of water scattered throughout the mountains. Among these are Lake Bomoseen and Emerald Lake in the southwestern part of the state, and Lakes Carmi and Memphremagog in the north.

▲ The Aurora Borealis, or Northern Lights, can be seen in the Vermont skies.

▶ Severe Weather

Weather conditions in Vermont can be extreme, and Vermont residents are known for their ability to overcome difficult winters. In 1816, the winter was so cold and lasted so long that a foot of snow fell in some towns as late as June 6. There were frosts in July and August, destroying crops and livestock on a massive scale.

The flood of 1927 was the worst in the state's history. The *Rutland Herald*, one of the state's leading newspapers, described the effects of the flood in its November 6 edition:

"Vermont's loss is today incalculable. Lives without number have been snuffed out. Property damage running into the millions has been caused. But Green Mountain folk still have their faith and this is the weapon with which they are striking back at Catastrophe."[1]

Economy

Vermont is well known for a variety of products and industries. Some industries, such as dairy farming and rock quarrying, date back more than a century. Others—electronics production, social services, and tourism, for example—developed during the twentieth century. Grain farming and lumber production have become less important in recent years.

▶ Vermont as Frontier

In its early days, Vermont resembled the western frontier. Much of the land was unsettled, and people moved there to farm and build their homes. As in the new western states and territories, Vermont's population grew rapidly in the early nineteenth century. Canals, factories, railroads, and roads

Shortly after Vermont gained ▶ statehood in 1791, people came to the state to clear the land for farming.

were built. Land was cleared and plowed for farms and mills.

However, it was hard for Vermont to compete with the larger western states. Many of these, such as Iowa and Kansas, were level and fertile. Vermont's small area and mostly-mountainous terrain could not produce the same amounts of grains and vegetables. Even forestry products, which had been important in Vermont for much of the eighteenth century, faded with the new competition from the West.

Manufacturing grew rapidly in Vermont after it became a state. Factories produced large quantities of woven fabrics and distilled beverages. These goods did not depend on the amount and/or quality of the land. Still, the rough terrain and harsh weather made it harder to ship them from Vermont than from other places.

▲ Covered with license plates from across the country, this shed in Vermont is certainly interesting.

Vermont was the fastest-growing state from the 1790s until the War of 1812. By the mid- to late nineteenth century, however, businesses in Vermont were growing much more slowly than in most of the country. This meant that the state attracted fewer people, and as a result, its population grew more slowly. Historian Charles T. Morrissey described the change:

> . . . between 1840 and 1850 [Vermont] was the slowest-growing state in the nation. The 314,120 [people] counted in 1850 grew by only 978 (0.3 percent) in the next decade. . . . Its population when the Civil War started was 315,098, and this increased by less than 50,000 by the time World War Two started. In one of those decades the state grew not at all: in two others . . . it actually lost population.[1]

Building on Strengths

Despite the state's problems, Vermont products and businesses did become successful, even famous. Vermont made good use of its natural climate and environment, and of the cleverness and determination of its people. Vermont farmers realized that dairy farming was best suited to the environment. Other agricultural products that were successful include apples, berries, honey, maple products, and pears.

Mining and quarrying flourished during the nineteenth century. Large-scale mining declined in later years. Quarrying, however, is still a major industry. It is less damaging to the land and an easier way to extract granite and marble from the earth. Vermont granite and marble are used around the world in building grave headstones, monuments, and other structures. The Rock of Ages Quarry Company and the Vermont Marble Company are the state's largest quarrying and mineral production companies.

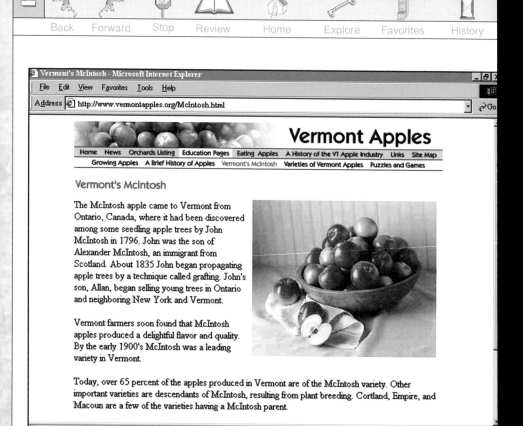

▲ *Over 65 percent of the apples grown in Vermont are McIntosh.*

Thadeus Fairbanks invented a new, more accurate platform scale in 1830. Rutland and St. Johnsbury soon became centers for the manufacture of industrial scales. Another Vermonter, Richard Smith Lawrence, devised a new way to assemble firearms. This led to large-scale production of guns in the town of Windsor. Many industrial companies copied the manufacturing methods used there.

Vermont also became a leading producer of machine tools and assembly line equipment. The town of Springfield is a major production center for such items.

The Modern Economy

Even with these economic successes, Vermont sometimes experienced hardship during the nineteenth and early twentieth centuries.

Vermont had been a favorite destination of tourists in the early nineteenth century, but its popularity declined as the years passed. The state tried hard to change this. Michael Sherman of the Vermont Historical Society described these efforts, saying: "Together with the railroads, the state government promoted tourism . . . through booklets and annual publications. . . . In 1911 Vermont created a Publicity Department, the nation's first state agency to promote tourism."[2]

Vermont Maple Syrup - Microsoft Internet Explorer

File Edit View Favorites Tools Help

Address http://www.americaslibrary.gov/pages/es_vt_syrup_1.html   Go

Home ★About this site ★Help   The Library of Congress

America's Story from America's Library   Meet Amazing Americans   Jump Back in Time   Explore the States   Join America at Play   See, Hear and Sing

Explore the States ▸ Vermont

Vermont Maple Syrup
Do you like pancakes with maple syrup? Did you know that Vermont produces more maple syrup than any other state in the United States?

The process used to make maple syrup is essentially the same one that Native Americans first used hundreds of years ago.

For four to six weeks in the winter or early spring, farmers collect the sweet-water sap of dormant sugar maple or black maple trees. The sap is extracted through tap holes, which are carefully drilled into the trees and fitted with spouts and buckets or the more modern and common method, plastic tubing. The sweet-water sap is then boiled in pans to evaporate the liquid. The sap only yields one-thirtieth to one-fiftieth the amount of syrup as the original quantity of sap.

Gathering sap from sugar trees for making maple syrup

Click for enlargement and credits

Internet

▲ *American Indians began making maple syrup hundreds of years ago. It remains one of Vermont's most important agricultural products.*

One invention gave Vermont tourism, and the tourists a boost. In the winter of 1934, a motorized ski tow began operating in the town of Stowe. A ski resort was soon built there on the slopes of Mount Mansfield. After the Great Depression and World War II, skiing exploded in popularity. By 2000, there were thirty-one ski resorts in the state, and Vermont became known around the world as a top ski area. Tourism became Vermont's third-largest industry, providing about 15 percent of the state's revenues.

Another key event was a statewide referendum in 1936. The people voted against building a multilane highway along the crest of the Green Mountains. This highway

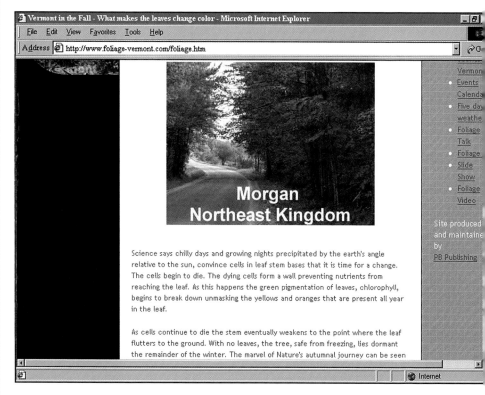

Tourists flock to Vermont during the autumn months to see the beautiful fall foliage.

would have brought money into the state. Jobs were badly needed during the Great Depression, and many states were eager for projects like this. Vermonters, though, voted against it by 58 percent to 42 percent. Over the years since 1936, Vermont has continued to take many steps to protect its land and environment from overdevelopment. As a result, much of Vermont is still wild forests, open plains, and farmland that make the state attractive to vacationers.

▶ Act 250

The ski industry and the environmentalists disagreed about development in the late 1960s. There were serious traffic jams in the resort areas. Construction of new buildings was causing soil erosion and problems with the water supply. The cost of property rose, as did the taxes residents had to pay.

Vermont residents knew that winter sports were important to their state economy. They realized that more visitors would mean more money for the state. On the other hand they worried that their state's natural beauty and historic qualities were being threatened.

New legislation was proposed to deal with the problem. According to the *New York Times*, "a state environmental control commission was appointed to supervise land development, particularly in the rapidly-growing ski areas of southern Vermont."[3]

Act 250 forced builders to plan for protection of water supplies and for higher levels of traffic. There were also measures to prevent erosion and make sure land was being used properly.

Developers and real estate workers were against Act 250. They said the act would hurt the strong economic

growth in Vermont. The state's residents had seen their personal income increase at the highest rate in the nation during the 1960s.

In spite of this opposition, the legislation was passed in April 1970 with strong support. Growth did slow after the passage of Act 250 but has remained steady during the last several decades.

High Technology, Health, and Education

High-tech companies, such as IBM and Digital Equipment, have established factories and facilities in the state. These businesses have been able to grow without hurting the environment and have helped to boost manufacturing in the

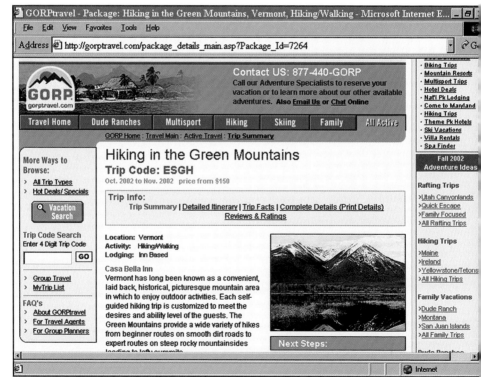

▲ Act 250 restricted construction in places such as Vermont's Green Mountains.

state. Manufacturing employs about 15 percent of Vermont's workers.

Health and social services are also important. Vermont has a long history of support for physical and mental health programs. The state spends more per person on these services than any other state. The Brattleboro Retreat, for example, was founded in 1834 and is still in operation. It has pioneered new ways to treat the mentally ill. About thirty thousand people currently work in health and social services in Vermont. They provide patients with health care, useful work programs, exercise activities, and recreation.

There are many colleges and universities in Vermont. The University of Vermont in Burlington is the largest, with about ten thousand students. Middlebury and Bennington colleges are well known for their art and literary programs. Champlain College is strong in business education, and Sterling College combines liberal arts with challenging outdoor adventures. World Learning, in Brattleboro, specializes in international relations and the study of foreign languages and cultures.

Government

Vermont's government is known as one of the most democratic and open in the nation.

A Democratic Tradition

The first Vermont constitution, passed in 1777, banned slavery and allowed all male citizens to vote. Vermont gained a reputation as a place where common people could easily take part in their government. The state has also benefited from leaders who have stayed closely in touch with the citizens they represent.

There is a story about a foreign official who visited Thomas Chittenden, Vermont's first governor. He arrived at the governor's mansion to find a man chopping firewood in the doorway. The official asked this man to hold his horse's reins. The visitor was stunned to learn that the man who had been chopping wood and was now looking after his horse, was in fact Governor Chittenden!

Organization

Like most states and the federal government, Vermont's government has three branches—legislative, executive, and judiciary. The executive branch includes the governor, lieutenant governor, secretary of state, and attorney general. These officials are elected for two-year terms.

The state legislature is divided into a house of representatives and a senate. Members of these houses also are elected to two-year terms. Every town in Vermont used to have one representative in the house. By the mid-twentieth century, there were 246 representatives. In 1965, federal courts decided that this system was unfair, because it gave small towns advantages over larger areas. The house was restructured, and now has 150 members. Each member represents about the same number of people. The senate has thirty members.

The supreme court is the highest court in the state. District courts deal with criminal cases. Superior courts deal with civil cases—family, property, and traffic problems, for example. Vermont also has an unusual kind of court: an environmental court that hears cases involving environmental protection.

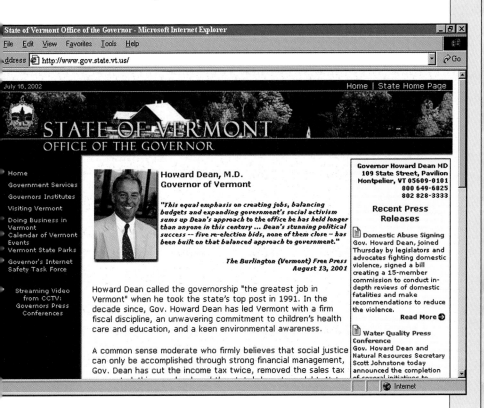

Dr. Howard Dean became governor of Vermont in 1991.

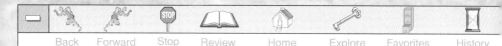

◀ *A covered bridge in Vermont.*

Town meetings are an important part of government in Vermont. On the first Tuesday of March each year, people meet in cities, towns, and villages. They elect local officials and discuss local topics such as how many houses and factories should be built, road and bridge repair, and funding for schools. Town meetings can last for hours, and discussions can become heated. One year, the people of Arlington had to choose to either repair the town's bridges or build a new grade school. There was not enough money to do both. Those who wanted to repair the bridges seemed likely to win. Then the local grocer spoke up for the school. Vermont historian Dorothy Canfield Fisher said his words were as "intense as the flame of a blowtorch." He asked the meeting, "What kind of a town would we rather have fifty years from now—a place where nitwit folks go back and forth over good bridges? Or a town which has always given its children a fair chance, and prepares them to hold their own in modern life?"[1] In the end, the people of Arlington chose to build the school.

▶ Independent and Unpredictable

In the famous presidential election of 1860, Abraham Lincoln ran against Stephen Douglas. Lincoln opposed slavery; Douglas supported slavery. Most Vermonters were strongly against slavery. So even though Douglas had been born in Vermont, the state voted for Lincoln by a landslide.

The Republican Party dominated state government and elections in Vermont from the middle of the nineteenth century to the middle of the twentieth century. Vermont Republicans, though, did not always agree with the rest of their party.

George Aiken is one of Vermont's most highly-respected politicians. He was elected governor in 1936. After two

Stephen A. Douglas Was Born - Microsoft Internet Explorer

File   Edit   View   Favorites   Tools   Help

Address ⬦ http://www.americaslibrary.gov/pages/jb_0423_litgiant_1_e.html   ⟳ Go

🌐 Internet

▲ *Stephen A. Douglas ran against Abraham Lincoln in the 1860 election.*

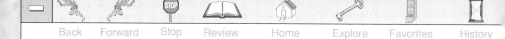
terms he became a senator, and served in Washington, D.C., for thirty-four years. He became one of the Senate's leading experts on agriculture and social services. These areas were not always of great interest to the Republican Party, but they were both important to Vermont residents. Aiken also opposed the Vietnam War, disagreeing with most of his fellow Republicans.

The Republicans began to lose power in Vermont in the late 1950s. A Democrat was elected governor in 1962. George Aiken left the Senate in 1975. He was then its most senior member. His replacement, Patrick Leahy, was the first Democratic senator from Vermont in 150 years. In 1991, Vermont elected an independent, Bernie Sanders, to the House of Representatives. An independent belongs to no political party.

For many years, Sanders was the only independent member of Congress. However, in 2001, fellow Vermonter Jim Jeffords joined him. Jeffords had been a Republican since first being elected a senator in 1988. He decided to leave the party and become an independent. He said he no longer agreed with some important Republican policies. His action meant the Republicans lost their majority in the Senate. Jeffords was both praised and criticized for this switch. His decision was typical of the political independence of Vermont's voters and public officials.

History

Archaeologists believe that the land that is now Vermont was first inhabited between 9000 and 7000 B.C. At that time a large body of water covered part of Vermont. The sea provided food for the people who lived there. As this sea receded, the early settlers moved away. There are signs that wandering groups of hunters and gatherers spent time in Vermont during the following centuries. Permanent farming settlements first appeared about A.D. 1300. These were inhabited by the Abenaki Indians, who lived mostly along the banks of what is now called Lake Champlain. The lake is named for the French explorer who visited the region hundreds of years later.

▶ The Europeans Arrive

French explorer Samuel de Champlain came to Vermont from Quebec in the early seventeenth century. He reported seeing a strange creature in the large lake on the state's northwest border. Local natives also had legends about such a creature. Stories about the Lake Champlain monster still exist today. The monster is nicknamed Champ, and is sometimes referred to as "the Loch Ness Monster of North America."[1]

Champlain led the way for French settlers. He became friendly with the American Indians in the Champlain Valley, and he set up successful fur trapping, hunting, and trade in the area. To build good relations with the Abenaki, he helped them fight their enemy, the Iroquois. In 1666,

the French built Fort Ste. Anne on Isle La Motte in Lake Champlain. French settlement gradually spread south through the Champlain Valley.

British settlers from southern New England and New York also ventured into Vermont. The first permanent British settlement was a military base called Fort Dummer. It was built in 1724 on the Connecticut River, just north of what is now Brattleboro. The fort's role was to defend Massachusetts against raids by American Indians from the north.

At this time, the French were friendly with the Abenaki and the Abenaki's allies, so the English formed alliances with the rival Iroquois nation.

▶ Early Wars

A series of conflicts took place between British and French settlers and their American Indian allies during the late seventeenth and eighteenth centuries. These struggles were part of a larger military rivalry between Britain and France. The two nations fought a series of wars elsewhere in New England and North America, and around the globe. The conflicts included King William's War in the 1690s, Queen Anne's War about ten years later, and the French and Indian War in the 1750s and 1760s. During these conflicts, both sides often used the Champlain Valley as a route of attack.

◀ *Samuel de Champlain.*

The British won the French and Indian War in 1763. This set the stage for a new conflict in Vermont. The colonies of New York and New Hampshire fought for control of territories around the Green Mountains.

The Green Mountain Boys

New York claimed all the land north of Massachusetts and east to the Connecticut River. New Hampshire governor Benning Wentworth, however, had already granted, or given, territory in that area to his friends and to New Hampshire residents. New York asked Britain to resolve the matter. The British courts sided with New York but did not want to take action to enforce this decision.

After the French and Indian War, the British gained all French and Spanish possessions east of the Mississippi. The green area is the land that Britain controlled prior to the war. In 1764, the land that is Vermont was part of the New York colony.

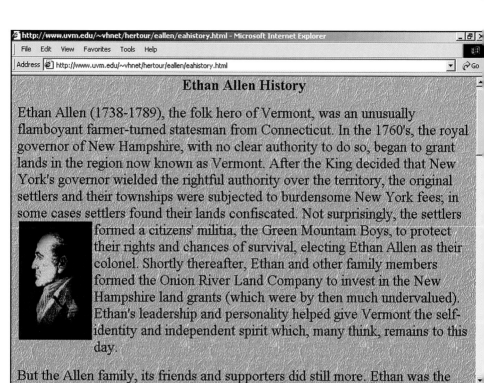

Ethan Allen History

Ethan Allen (1738-1789), the folk hero of Vermont, was an unusually flamboyant farmer-turned statesman from Connecticut. In the 1760's, the royal governor of New Hampshire, with no clear authority to do so, began to grant lands in the region now known as Vermont. After the King decided that New York's governor wielded the rightful authority over the territory, the original settlers and their townships were subjected to burdensome New York fees; in some cases settlers found their lands confiscated. Not surprisingly, the settlers formed a citizens' militia, the Green Mountain Boys, to protect their rights and chances of survival, electing Ethan Allen as their colonel. Shortly thereafter, Ethan and other family members formed the Onion River Land Company to invest in the New Hampshire land grants (which were by then much undervalued). Ethan's leadership and personality helped give Vermont the self-identity and independent spirit which, many think, remains to this day.

But the Allen family, its friends and supporters did still more. Ethan was the

Done   Internet

▲ *Ethan Allen was elected to be the first colonel of the Green Mountain Boys.*

The people who had settled in what were called "the New Hampshire Grants" were unhappy about being part of the Colony of New York, and some rebelled. One of these was Ethan Allen, who organized a group called the Green Mountain Boys. These men whipped up opposition to the "Yorkers."

The actions of the Green Mountain Boys are explained in this passage: "In the early 1770s, Green Mountain Boys controlled the lands west of the mountains as roving rangers, despite the efforts of New Yorkers to combat them. The principal targets of the Green Mountain Boys were New York sheriffs, surveyors, and landjobbers [real estate agents]."[2]

The New Hampshire Grant holders resisted attempts to remove them from their land. One of the most dramatic events in this conflict was the Westminster Massacre. In this incident, New York forces killed two Grant holders who were part of a force occupying a courthouse. Word of the incident brought more than five hundred local people to the courthouse. They drove off the Yorkers and freed other Grant holders who were being held prisoner.

▶ Revolutionary War

The attention of the Green Mountain Boys and others in Vermont soon turned to the Revolutionary War, which started in 1775. Allen and the Green Mountain Boys joined the fight for independence, helping to defeat the British in important battles. The Green Mountain Boys played a major role at Fort Ticonderoga, Crown Point, and other battles in the Champlain Valley.

Only one Revolutionary War battle took place on Vermont soil, at the village of Hubbarton. American forces who were returning from an attack on Canada met and fought advancing British troops.

The Battle of Bennington, in 1777, is considered a major step toward American victory. However, it was actually fought in the town of Hoosic, New York, west of Bennington. The battle is so named, because British troops were trying to capture weapons and supplies that were stored in Bennington. A force of Green Mountain Boys led by Seth Warner beat back the British.

The people of the Grants were afraid the Continental Congress would divide the Grants among their neighboring states. So they declared themselves a separate state in

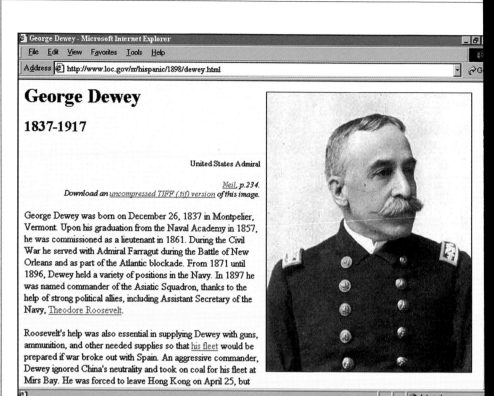

George Dewey - Microsoft Internet Explorer

File   Edit   View   Favorites   Tools   Help

Address http://www.loc.gov/rr/hispanic/1898/dewey.html

George Dewey

1837-1917

United States Admiral

Neil, p.234.
Download an _uncompressed TIFF (.tif) version_ of this image.

George Dewey was born on December 26, 1837 in Montpelier, Vermont. Upon his graduation from the Naval Academy in 1857, he was commissioned as a lieutenant in 1861. During the Civil War he served with Admiral Farragut during the Battle of New Orleans and as part of the Atlantic blockade. From 1871 until 1896, Dewey held a variety of positions in the Navy. In 1897 he was named commander of the Asiatic Squadron, thanks to the help of strong political allies, including Assistant Secretary of the Navy, Theodore Roosevelt.

Roosevelt's help was also essential in supplying Dewey with guns, ammunition, and other needed supplies so that his fleet would be prepared if war broke out with Spain. An aggressive commander, Dewey ignored China's neutrality and took on coal for his fleet at Mirs Bay. He was forced to leave Hong Kong on April 25, but

Internet

Admiral George Dewey, a key player in the Spanish-American War, was born in Vermont.

1777. At first, this new state was called New Connecticut. This was changed to Vermont—from the French for "green mountain"—in June 1778.

In 1779, Vermont went even further and declared itself an independent country. However, Vermont residents continued to support the Revolutionary War. After the war ended, in 1783, disagreements with other states were resolved, and Vermont became the fourteenth state in 1791.

▶ War of 1812

There was also major military action in the Champlain Valley during the War of 1812. British vessels bombarded the city of Burlington. A fleet of United States ships was built in Vermont in just six weeks. These ships played a major role in the United States victory in the Battle of Plattsburgh, fought in New York, just across Lake Champlain.

Additional Contributions

In the Civil War, Vermont sent more than 10 percent of its total population to fight on the Union side. It suffered the highest casualty rate of any Union state. Vermont was also where the northernmost action of the Civil War took place. This was a raid launched by a band of Confederates who sneaked south from Canada in October 1864. They robbed banks, terrorized citizens, and damaged property before fleeing back north.

The Spanish-American War was fought in the Caribbean Sea and South Pacific Ocean, thousands of miles from Vermont. Two Vermonters, though, Admiral George Dewey and Admiral George Clark, played important roles in this conflict, leading United States forces to victories in important battles.

Vermonters have made other kinds of contributions to history. Besides George Aiken, Bernie Sanders, and Jim Jeffords, other notable Vermont officeholders include Matthew Lyon and Warren Austin. Matthew Lyon is most famous for brawling with Connecticut's Roger Griswold in the U.S. House Chamber. He was arrested and jailed on questionable charges by his political opponents. Lyon was reelected by a large majority while in prison in 1798. Warren Austin gained fame as an early supporter of United States involvement in World War II. He served as a senator from Vermont before being chosen as the first United States ambassador to the United Nations in the 1940s.

▷ An Eye to the Environment and Social Progress

Vermont has taken many legal actions in the past century that are of great historical importance. Environmental decisions include the passage of Act 250. Vermont was also one of the first states to require recycling of soft drink containers.

Vermont has taken important actions on social issues. The state has been a leader in granting civil rights and equality among its citizens. In 1998, the state passed Act 60. This aims to make education more equal among rich and poor. School tax money will be shared across the state. People in some wealthier towns do not like this. They have

▲ Although more roads are being built in Vermont, its citizens have taken actions to protect the environment.

tried to stop paying public school taxes, and by sending their children to private schools.

More people are moving to Vermont from big cities. The state has an increasingly international feel, especially around the major ski areas. There are many new and innovative businesses. It is therefore likely that Vermont will continue to be progressive and make bold decisions in the future. Vermont's spirit of independence lives on.

Chapter 1. The Green Mountain State

1. U.S. Census Bureau, "States Ranked by Population," *Census 2000*, April 2, 2000, <http://www.census.gov/population/cen2000/phc-t2/tab01.html> (August 27, 2002).

Chapter 2. Land and Climate

1. "Entire State Suffers Blow," *Rutland Herald*, vol. 74, No. 266, November 6, 1927, p. 1.

Chapter 3. Economy

1. Charles T. Morrissey, *Vermont: A History* (New York: W.W. Norton & Company, 1981), p. 107.

2. Michael. Sherman, "Rails, Trails, and Automobiles: Tourism in Vermont," *We Vermonters: Perspectives on the Past* (Montpelier: Vermont Historical Society, 1992), p. 257.

3. "Vermont Legislature Passes Environmental Control Bills," *The New York Times*, April 6, 1970, p. 31.

Chapter 4. Government

1. Dorothy Canfield Fisher, quoted in Charles T. Morrissey, *Vermont: A History* (New York: W.W. Norton & Company, 1981), p. 175. Originally in *Memories of My Home Town* (Arlington, Vt.: Arlington Historical Society, 1955), p. 101.

Chapter 5. History

1. Mark Chorvinsky, "Champ of Lake Champlain," *Strange Magazine*, 1995, <http://www.strangemag.com/champ.html> (August 27, 2002).

2. John Duffy and Vincent Feeney. *Vermont: An Illustrated History* (Sun Valley, Calif.: American Historical Press, 2000), p. 52.

Aronson, Virginia. Ethan Allen, *Revolutionary Hero.* Philadelphia: Chelsea House, 2001.

Aylesworth, Thomas and Virginia. *Northern New England.* New York: Chelsea House, 1996.

Crump, Donald J. *New England: Land of Scenic Splendor.* Washington, D.C.: National Geographic Society, 1989.

Elish, Dan. *Vermont.* New York: Benchmark Books/Marshall Cavendish, 1997.

Graham, Amy. *Calvin Coolidge.* Berkeley Heights, N.J.: MyReportLinks.com Books, 2002.

Greenberg, Keith Elliot. *Ben & Jerry: Ice Cream for Everyone!* Woodbridge, Conn.: Blackbirch Press, 1994.

Heinrichs, Ann. *Vermont.* New York: Children's Press, 2001.

Pringle, Lawrence. *The Environmental Movement: From Its Roots to the Challenges of a New Century.* New York: HarperCollins, 2000.

Thompson, Kathleen. *Vermont.* Austin, Tex.: Raintree/Steck Vaughn, 1996.